Adult MAD LIBS®

The world's greatest _wedding_ game

Just Married Mad Libs

by Molly Reisner

Mad Libs
An Imprint of Penguin Random House

MAD LIBS
An Imprint of Penguin Random House LLC

Concept created by Roger Price & Leonard Stern

Published by Mad Libs,
an imprint of Penguin Random House LLC,
345 Hudson Street, New York, New York 10014.
Printed in the USA.

ISBN 9780843180008
10

INSTRUCTIONS

The world's greatest *wedding* game

MAD LIBS® is a game for people who don't like games!
It can be played by one, two, three, four, or forty.

• RIDICULOUSLY SIMPLE DIRECTIONS

In this book, you'll find stories containing blank spaces where words are left out. One player, the READER, selects one of the stories. The READER shouldn't tell anyone what the story is about. Instead, the READER should ask the other players, the WRITERS, to give words to fill in the blank spaces in the story.

• TO PLAY

The READER asks each WRITER in turn to call out words—adjectives or nouns or whatever the spaces call for—and uses them to fill in the blank spaces in the story. The result is your very own MAD LIBS! Then, when the READER reads the completed MAD LIBS to the other players, they will discover they have written a story that is fantastic, screamingly funny, shocking, silly, crazy, or just plain dumb— depending on the words each WRITER called out.

• EXAMPLE (*Before* and *After*)

"_____!" he said _____
        EXCLAMATION   ADVERB

as he jumped into his convertible _____ and
                                          NOUN

drove off with his _____ wife.
                          ADJECTIVE

"*Ouch*!" he said *stupidly*
        EXCLAMATION   ADVERB

as he jumped into his convertible *cat* and
                                          NOUN

drove off with his *brave* wife.
                          ADJECTIVE

The world's greatest *wedding* game

In case you have forgotten what adjectives, adverbs, nouns, and verbs are, here is a quick review:

An **ADJECTIVE** describes something or somebody. *Lumpy, soft, ugly, messy,* and *short* are adjectives.

An **ADVERB** tells how something is done. It modifies a verb and usually ends in "ly." *Modestly, stupidly, greedily,* and *carefully* are adverbs.

A **NOUN** is the name of a person, place, or thing. *Sidewalk, umbrella, bridle, bathtub,* and *nose* are nouns.

A **VERB** is an action word. *Run, pitch, jump,* and *swim* are verbs. Put the verbs in past tense if the directions say **PAST TENSE.** *Ran, pitched, jumped,* and *swam* are verbs in the past tense.

When we ask for **A PLACE,** we mean any sort of place: a country or city (*Spain, Cleveland*) or a room (*bathroom, kitchen*).

An **EXCLAMATION** or **SILLY WORD** is any sort of funny sound, gasp, grunt, or outcry, like *Wow!, Ouch!, Whomp!, Ick!,* and *Gadzooks!*

When we ask for specific words, like a **NUMBER,** a **COLOR,** an **ANIMAL,** or a **PART OF THE BODY,** we mean a word that is one of those things, like *seven, blue, horse,* or *head.*

When we ask for a **PLURAL,** it means more than one. For example, *cat* pluralized is *cats.*

Adult
MAD LIBS®
THE COMFORT ZONE
The world's greatest _wedding_ game

MAD LIBS® is fun to play with friends, but you can also play it by yourself! To begin with, DO NOT look at the story on the page below. Fill in the blanks on this page with the words called for. Then, using the words you have selected, fill in the blank spaces in the story. Now you've created your own hilarious MAD LIBS® game!

PART OF THE BODY _tongue_

VERB _Slither_

ADJECTIVE _Pink_

NOUN _bunny_

COLOR _blue_

ARTICLE OF CLOTHING (PLURAL) _panties_

NOUN _Surfboard_

ADJECTIVE _smooth_

PART OF THE BODY _thigh_

VERB ENDING IN "ING" _flopping_

PLURAL NOUN _eyes_

VERB ENDING IN "ING" _yelling_

PLURAL NOUN _balls_

NOUN _tuxedo_

PLURAL NOUN _mops_

PART OF THE BODY _elbow_

Now that you're hitched, are you and your sweet _____

PART OF THE BODY

letting it all _____ loose? You know you're entering The

VERB

Comfort Zone when . . . You both eat everything in sight, now

that you don't have to look _____ for wedding photos. A

ADJECTIVE

romantic night at home used to be a/an _____-lit dinner

NOUN

for two and a bottle of _____ wine, but now consists of your

COLOR

comfiest _____, the remote _____, and his-and-

ARTICLE OF CLOTHING (PLURAL)   NOUN

hers recliners. Not to mention a large tray of sweet and _____

ADJECTIVE

snacks within _____'s reach. _____ in the bathroom

PART OF THE BODY   VERB ENDING IN "ING"

in front of your beloved is no big deal. Picking the _____ out

PLURAL NOUN

of your nose is not a private event, and _____ wind in each

VERB ENDING IN "ING"

other's company is completely commonplace. You used to devour

each other's _____ like the world was ending. Now? A roll

PLURAL NOUN

in the _____ is nice, but catching up on your DVR'd shows

NOUN

is just as important. Speaking of rolls, you have matching muffin

_____. What's the rush to get back to the gym? After all, you

PLURAL NOUN

worked your _____ off to reach The Comfort Zone!

PART OF THE BODY

Adult MAD LIBS® THANK-YOU NOTE GENERATOR

The world's greatest *wedding* game

MAD LIBS® is fun to play with friends, but you can also play it by yourself! To begin with, DO NOT look at the story on the page below. Fill in the blanks on this page with the words called for. Then, using the words you have selected, fill in the blank spaces in the story. Now you've created your own hilarious MAD LIBS® game!

ADJECTIVE _____

ADJECTIVE _____

NOUN _____

PART OF THE BODY _____

NOUN _____

PART OF THE BODY _____

VERB (PAST TENSE) _____

ADJECTIVE _____

A PLACE _____

NOUN _____

NUMBER _____

VERB _____

Adult
MAD LIBS® THANK-YOU NOTE GENERATOR

The world's greatest _wedding_ game

Dear [Insert Name of Wedding Guest here],

Thank you so much for the thoughtful and _____ gift you
                                         ADJECTIVE

gave us. It's _____ and just what we wanted! We were so
              ADJECTIVE

thrilled you were able to be a part of our once-in-a/an-_____
                                                          NOUN

celebration. Your presence truly filled my _____ with joy. Our
                                            PART OF THE BODY

wedding was a dream come true, just like a/an _____! The
                                              NOUN

day flew by in a blink of a/an _____.
                               PART OF THE BODY

We wish we could do it all over again, except next time maybe

we'll have _____ our first dance moves a little more! So far,
           VERB (PAST TENSE)

wedded bliss has been full of _____ times and laughter. We
                              ADJECTIVE

just got back from two weeks in gorgeous St. _____ at an all-
                                             A PLACE

inclusive _____. I think we spent _____% of our time
          NOUN   NUMBER

at the buffet!

Thanks again for the gift and hope to _____ up with you
                                      VERB

soon!

Love, Us

MAD LIBS® is fun to play with friends, but you can also play it by yourself! To begin with, DO NOT look at the story on the page below. Fill in the blanks on this page with the words called for. Then, using the words you have selected, fill in the blank spaces in the story. Now you've created your own hilarious MAD LIBS® game!

NOUN _____

ADJECTIVE _____

PART OF THE BODY _____

NOUN _____

PART OF THE BODY _____

ANIMAL _____

VERB ENDING IN "ING" _____

NOUN _____

NOUN _____

NOUN _____

FIRST NAME (FEMALE) _____

NOUN _____

VERB _____

NOUN _____

VERB ENDING IN "ING" _____

NOUN _____

COLOR _____

A/An _____-of-honor gets into _____ water with
                NOUN   ADJECTIVE

a bride over unflattering photos she uploaded onto _____-
                                              PART OF THE BODY

book. Check out their online war of words!

Bride: Can you un-post your pictures from my wedding? In one

photo there's a piece of _____ stuck between my front
                          NOUN

teeth. And then there's one of my sweetie with sweat pouring off

his _____ as he does the _____ dance. He looks
    PART OF THE BODY   ANIMAL

insane. Need I mention the picture of me _____ in the
                                          VERB ENDING IN "ING"

toilet with my huge _____ hoisted up? And for the love of
                    NOUN

_____, take down the ones from the after-party of people
    NOUN

doing _____ stands!
       NOUN

_____: Okay, _____-zilla, you need to _____
FIRST NAME (FEMALE)   NOUN   VERB

out. The bathroom one I get. My bad! But the others are so vibrant

and full of _____. I'm going to leave them up. Don't hate me!
            NOUN

Bride: In that case, I have a picture of you French _____ my
                                                      VERB ENDING IN "ING"

_____-in-law. Hmmm, should I add this to your wall? And
    NOUN

yes, this is _____-mail!
              COLOR

Adult MAD LIBS®

The world's greatest *wedding* game

HONEYMOON SWOON

MAD LIBS® is fun to play with friends, but you can also play it by yourself! To begin with, DO NOT look at the story on the page below. Fill in the blanks on this page with the words called for. Then, using the words you have selected, fill in the blank spaces in the story. Now you've created your own hilarious MAD LIBS® game!

NOUN _____

ADJECTIVE _____

NOUN _____

NUMBER _____

VERB ENDING IN "ING" _____

ADJECTIVE _____

COLOR _____

ADJECTIVE _____

ADJECTIVE _____

EXCLAMATION _____

PART OF THE BODY _____

NOUN _____

PLURAL NOUN _____

NOUN _____

VERB ENDING IN "ING" _____

VERB (PAST TENSE) _____

PLURAL NOUN _____

ADJECTIVE _____

Adult MAD LIBS

HONEYMOON SWOON

The world's greatest _wedding_ game

I just got back from my honeymoon in the _____
                                               NOUN

Islands, and we had such a/an _____ time! Besides a few
                                   ADJECTIVE

tropical _____ showers, the weather was perfect. Our
              NOUN

_____-star hotel suite had a private outdoor hot tub and mini
NUMBER

_____ pool. I think there was something _____ in
VERB ENDING IN "ING"   ADJECTIVE

the water because my skin broke out in a/an _____, bumpy
                                  COLOR

rash. No worries, though—everything looks _____ with a tan!
                                ADJECTIVE

The ocean was as _____ as bath water and crystal-clear. Aaah!
               ADJECTIVE

And the food—_____! It was _____-watering. My
              EXCLAMATION   PART OF THE BODY

husband and I tried all the local delicacies like fried _____
                                            NOUN

and steamed _____. Yum! Unfortunately, he came down with
              PLURAL NOUN

a case of _____-poisoning so we didn't go zip_____
              NOUN   VERB ENDING IN "ING"

like we'd planned. For two whole days he _____ his guts out,
                                    VERB (PAST TENSE)

poor thing!

When he felt better, we celebrated with cocktails and made wishes

on all the shooting _____ in the sky. I wished for a long and
                            PLURAL NOUN

_____ marriage, of course!
ADJECTIVE

Adult MAD LIBS — THE BIG NIGHT

The world's greatest _wedding_ game

MAD LIBS® is fun to play with friends, but you can also play it by yourself! To begin with, DO NOT look at the story on the page below. Fill in the blanks on this page with the words called for. Then, using the words you have selected, fill in the blank spaces in the story. Now you've created your own hilarious MAD LIBS® game!

NOUN	Dildo
NOUN	Nose Ring
NOUN	Frozen Hotdog
NOUN	Peach
TYPE OF LIQUID	Rum Runner
NUMBER	17
PART OF THE BODY (PLURAL)	toes
VERB	scoot
VERB ENDING IN "ING"	begging
PLURAL NOUN	thighs
PART OF THE BODY (PLURAL)	Boobs
VERB	sex
NOUN	gel
PLURAL NOUN	cups
NOUN	lube
PLURAL NOUN	sheets
VERB ENDING IN "ING"	coming
VERB ENDING IN "ING"	screaming

Adult
MAD LIBS®
THE BIG NIGHT

The world's greatest _wedding_ game

Your first night as a married _____ is supposed to be the most
_{NOUN}

romantic night ever, right? After a picture-perfect wedding, the eager

_____ carries his new _____ across the threshold into
_{NOUN}   _{NOUN}

a dimly lit bedroom. _____ petals are scattered across the
_{NOUN}

floor and a bottle of _____ awaits. The whirlwind of the day
_{TYPE OF LIQUID}

is over, leaving just the _____ of you, alone, finally!
_{NUMBER}

You both can't wait to get your _____ all over each other.
_{PART OF THE BODY (PLURAL)}

Sounds nice, right? Sorry to _____ your bubble, but after
_{VERB}

an exhausting day of _____ with your guests, smiling for
_{VERB ENDING IN "ING"}

_____, and dancing your _____ off, you probably
_{PLURAL NOUN}   _{PART OF THE BODY (PLURAL)}

won't even have the energy to _____ your teeth!
_{VERB}

Try not to be upset if your new spouse would rather hit the

_____ than rip your _____ off. But that doesn't mean
_{NOUN}   _{PLURAL NOUN}

you have to throw romance completely out the _____. A cozy
_{NOUN}

cuddle in your birthday _____ can be just as wonderful as a
_{PLURAL NOUN}

full-on love _____ session. And just think, you have the rest
_{VERB ENDING IN "ING"}

of your life to spend _____ with your new husband or wife!
_{VERB ENDING IN "ING"}

MAD LIBS® is fun to play with friends, but you can also play it by yourself! To begin with, DO NOT look at the story on the page below. Fill in the blanks on this page with the words called for. Then, using the words you have selected, fill in the blank spaces in the story. Now you've created your own hilarious MAD LIBS® game!

ADJECTIVE _____

VERB ENDING IN "ING" _____

NOUN _____

VERB _____

EXCLAMATION _____

ADJECTIVE _____

PLURAL NOUN _____

PLURAL NOUN _____

PART OF THE BODY _____

NOUN _____

NOUN _____

ADJECTIVE _____

VERB ENDING IN "ING" _____

VERB ENDING IN "ING" _____

PLURAL NOUN _____

ADJECTIVE _____

Are you feeling _____ now that your wedding is over?
<small>ADJECTIVE</small>

Do you find yourself _____ every morning, wishing you
<small>VERB ENDING IN "ING"</small>

still had _____ colors to pick out? Are you pining for a
<small>NOUN</small>

"to-_____" list of wedding tasks to tackle on the sly at
<small>VERB</small>

work? If you answered yes, then say "_____" to post-nuptial
<small>EXCLAMATION</small>

depression with these _____ tips!
<small>ADJECTIVE</small>

Keep busy planning something else. How about an anniversary

trip away or a dinner party with your best _____? Even
<small>PLURAL NOUN</small>

better, offer to help your newly engaged _____ with their
<small>PLURAL NOUN</small>

wedding plans! They'll be grateful to get advice from someone who's

just been _____-deep in _____ arrangements and
<small>PART OF THE BODY</small>   <small>NOUN</small>

_____ tastings.
<small>NOUN</small>

It's important to set a/an _____ goal for yourself. Start
<small>ADJECTIVE</small>

_____ for that marathon! Or take those bread-_____
<small>VERB ENDING IN "ING"</small>   <small>VERB ENDING IN "ING"</small>

classes you've been wanting to try. Whatever you decide, once you set

your _____ on a new journey, then your post-wedding blues
<small>PLURAL NOUN</small>

should disappear into _____ air!
<small>ADJECTIVE</small>

Adult MAD LIBS® — MONEY MATTERS

The world's greatest *wedding* game

MAD LIBS® is fun to play with friends, but you can also play it by yourself! To begin with, DO NOT look at the story on the page below. Fill in the blanks on this page with the words called for. Then, using the words you have selected, fill in the blank spaces in the story. Now you've created your own hilarious MAD LIBS® game!

PART OF THE BODY (PLURAL) _____

ADJECTIVE _____

VERB _____

ADJECTIVE _____

PLURAL NOUN _____

PLURAL NOUN _____

PLURAL NOUN _____

ADJECTIVE _____

NOUN _____

NOUN _____

VERB ENDING IN "ING" _____

NOUN _____

NOUN _____

ADJECTIVE _____

ADJECTIVE _____

NOUN _____

PART OF THE BODY _____

When you're head over _____ in love, who wants to talk
<small>PART OF THE BODY (PLURAL)</small>

about money matters? It's not the most _____ topic, but
<small>ADJECTIVE</small>

it's an important thing to discuss before you _____ the
<small>VERB</small>

knot. After all, disagreements over how your _____-earned
<small>ADJECTIVE</small>

cash is spent can lead to some major marital _____! Don't
<small>PLURAL NOUN</small>

let arguments over dollars and _____ get in the way of
<small>PLURAL NOUN</small>

your newlywed bliss. Learn how to tackle your joint _____
<small>PLURAL NOUN</small>

as a team! First, be _____ with each other about your
<small>ADJECTIVE</small>

money mishaps. Do you have a giant _____ loan or bad
<small>NOUN</small>

_____ report? 'Fess up! Next, work on _____ any
<small>NOUN</small> <small>VERB ENDING IN "ING"</small>

debt and consult a financial _____ for advice. Trying to save
<small>NOUN</small>

for your first _____ or a/an _____ set of wheels?
<small>NOUN</small> <small>ADJECTIVE</small>

Determine what your _____-term goals are, then budget your
<small>ADJECTIVE</small>

Benjamins to make your _____ a reality! After all, financial
<small>NOUN</small>

harmony is one of the _____-bones of a healthy marriage!
<small>PART OF THE BODY</small>

MAD LIBS® is fun to play with friends, but you can also play it by yourself! To begin with, DO NOT look at the story on the page below. Fill in the blanks on this page with the words called for. Then, using the words you have selected, fill in the blank spaces in the story. Now you've created your own hilarious MAD LIBS® game!

VERB (PAST TENSE) _____

PART OF THE BODY (PLURAL) _____

PLURAL NOUN _____

PLURAL NOUN _____

ADJECTIVE _____

TYPE OF LIQUID _____

ADJECTIVE _____

NOUN _____

ADVERB _____

ADJECTIVE _____

NOUN _____

ADJECTIVE _____

NOUN _____

NOUN _____

COLOR _____

Adult MAD LIBS®

The world's greatest _wedding_ game

VOW TO COMMUNICATE

Just because you've _____ down the aisle, it doesn't mean

VERB (PAST TENSE)

you're able to read each other's _____. After saying your

PART OF THE BODY (PLURAL)

"I dos", say these vows to keep the _____ of communication

PLURAL NOUN

wide open!

- I promise to tell you when I'm annoyed, like when you drop

  your _____ _by_ the hamper but not _in_ the hamper. Same

PLURAL NOUN

  goes for when you leave half-_____ glasses of

ADJECTIVE

  _____ in every room.

TYPE OF LIQUID

- I promise not to be _____-aggressive when we have

ADJECTIVE

  a/an _____.

NOUN

- I promise to share my thoughts _____, even when I'm

ADVERB

  super _____ that your ex-_____ is still texting you.

ADJECTIVE ⎯ NOUN

- I promise to let you know when I'm in a/an _____ mood

ADJECTIVE

  because of my boss being a total _____. Or when it's

NOUN

  "that time of the month" and I'm a raging _____.

NOUN

- More than anything, I promise to always tell the truth, unless a

  harmless _____ lie would make things better!

COLOR

MAD LIBS® is fun to play with friends, but you can also play it by yourself! To begin with, DO NOT look at the story on the page below. Fill in the blanks on this page with the words called for. Then, using the words you have selected, fill in the blank spaces in the story. Now you've created your own hilarious MAD LIBS® game!

NOUN _____

PLURAL NOUN _____

PART OF THE BODY _____

NOUN _____

VERB ENDING IN "ING" _____

ADVERB _____

NOUN _____

ADJECTIVE _____

NUMBER _____

NOUN _____

ADJECTIVE _____

VERB ENDING IN "ING" _____

NOUN _____

PLURAL NOUN _____

NOUN _____

PLURAL NOUN _____

VERB _____

ADJECTIVE _____

HONEY'S HABITS

Is the thought of putting the _____ seat down until the end
                                    NOUN

of time sending _____ down your spine? Does twisting the
                    PLURAL NOUN

_____-paste cap back on every night turn your _____
PART OF THE BODY   NOUN

upside down? Are you day-_____ about building your own
                          VERB ENDING IN "ING"

wing in the house? Learn how to _____ nip your partner's
                                      ADVERB

pesky habits in the bud! First, accept that there are some things you

just can't change about your _____-bear. And don't forget that
                                NOUN

_____ habits die hard! It's scientifically proven that it takes
  ADJECTIVE

_____ weeks to begin a new routine. That said, most people
  NUMBER

respond to the oldest trick in the _____—_____
                                      NOUN   ADJECTIVE

reinforcement! Whining and _____ to get your way will
                            VERB ENDING IN "ING"

only breed negative energy. Plus, it'll make you feel like a broken

_____. Instead, shower your sweetie with _____ every
  NOUN   PLURAL NOUN

time progress is made. Say things like, "I appreciate that you emptied

the _____-washer," or a simple "Thanks for cleaning the
      NOUN

_____ out of the gutter" might _____ like a charm.
  PLURAL NOUN   VERB

Keep it up and soon you'll have a home, _____ home!
                                          ADJECTIVE

MAD LIBS® is fun to play with friends, but you can also play it by yourself! To begin with, DO NOT look at the story on the page below. Fill in the blanks on this page with the words called for. Then, using the words you have selected, fill in the blank spaces in the story. Now you've created your own hilarious MAD LIBS® game!

FIRST NAME (FEMALE) _____

ADJECTIVE _____

NOUN _____

PLURAL NOUN _____

PART OF THE BODY (PLURAL) _____

A PLACE _____

COLOR _____

NOUN _____

NOUN _____

NOUN _____

NOUN _____

PLURAL NOUN _____

PART OF THE BODY _____

VERB ENDING IN "ING" _____

NOUN _____

VERB _____

ADJECTIVE _____

A phone call between a mother-in-law and her son's new wife:

"Hi, dear. It's me, _____! Oh, is this not a/an _____
      FIRST NAME (FEMALE)   ADJECTIVE

time to talk? I just wanted to make sure we have our daily telephone

_____! You can spare a few _____ for little old *moi*,
  NOUN   PLURAL NOUN

right? My son's just too busy to chat with me every day, but I know

you've got more time on your _____ since you work from
             PART OF THE BODY (PLURAL)

(the) _____. I was thinking we should start a tradition! I
    A PLACE

would be tickled _____ if we had a standing _____
        COLOR   NOUN

date on Fridays. Yes, of course, check your _____, but I
                  NOUN

just know my one and only _____ would love the idea.
         NOUN

He is a mama's _____ after all! He never could cut those
      NOUN

apron _____, bless his _____. And I wouldn't
   PLURAL NOUN   PART OF THE BODY

want him to! What's that? You really need to go pick up your dry

_____? Well, bring me along! We can chat while you drive
  VERB ENDING IN "ING"

the _____. I want to _____ your ear off about me
    NOUN   VERB

moving in with you two in the _____ future. Hello? I think
            ADJECTIVE

we got disconnected. Guess I'll have to call you back!"

The world's greatest _wedding_ game

MAD LIBS® is fun to play with friends, but you can also play it by yourself! To begin with, DO NOT look at the story on the page below. Fill in the blanks on this page with the words called for. Then, using the words you have selected, fill in the blank spaces in the story. Now you've created your own hilarious MAD LIBS® game!

PLURAL NOUN _____

NOUN _____

PART OF THE BODY _____

VERB _____

VERB ENDING IN "ING" _____

COLOR _____

ADJECTIVE _____

NOUN _____

ADJECTIVE _____

NOUN _____

PLURAL NOUN _____

VERB ENDING IN "ING" _____

ADJECTIVE _____

A PLACE _____

ADJECTIVE _____

ADJECTIVE _____

NOUN _____

So you're at a bar for _____' night out, and a really
<small>PLURAL NOUN</small>

cute _____ catches your _____. Before you can
<small>NOUN</small> <small>PART OF THE BODY</small>

_____ twice, you're making small talk with a stranger and it's
<small>VERB</small>

fun! All the while, you might be asking yourself, is a little harmless

_____ all that bad? Look out for these _____
<small>VERB ENDING IN "ING"</small> <small>COLOR</small>

flags to keep chit-chat from crossing the line into _____
<small>ADJECTIVE</small>

territory: First, be upfront about your status as a taken _____
<small>NOUN</small>

because you don't want to give this hottie any _____ ideas.
<small>ADJECTIVE</small>

Obviously, don't give out your _____ number. Or dish any
<small>NOUN</small>

_____ about your marriage. And for _____ out
<small>PLURAL NOUN</small> <small>VERB ENDING IN "ING"</small>

loud, reign in any _____ innuendo if the conversation takes
<small>ADJECTIVE</small>

a steamy turn! Even if that third _____ Iced Tea tells you to
<small>A PLACE</small>

keep it up. Imagine how _____ you'd feel if the tables were
<small>ADJECTIVE</small>

turned! The best plan? Establish your own rules with your sweetie

about flirting with members of the _____ sex. That way you
<small>ADJECTIVE</small>

won't be caught in a sticky _____!
<small>NOUN</small>

Adult
MAD LIBS BLING 101

The world's greatest *wedding* game

MAD LIBS® is fun to play with friends, but you can also play it by yourself! To begin with, DO NOT look at the story on the page below. Fill in the blanks on this page with the words called for. Then, using the words you have selected, fill in the blank spaces in the story. Now you've created your own hilarious MAD LIBS® game!

NOUN _____

NUMBER _____

ADJECTIVE _____

VERB _____

PLURAL NOUN _____

ADJECTIVE _____

NOUN _____

NUMBER _____

NOUN _____

PART OF THE BODY _____

ADVERB _____

TYPE OF LIQUID _____

NOUN _____

PLURAL NOUN _____

PLURAL NOUN _____

ADVERB _____

NOUN _____

ANIMAL _____

Adult MAD LIBS · BLING 101

The world's greatest _wedding_ game

A diamond is a/an _____'s best friend, right? Whether it's a
NOUN

_____-karat rock or _____ zirconia, you want your
NUMBER   ADJECTIVE

ring to sparkle and _____! With these tips, learn how to
VERB

make sure your gems shine brighter than a thousand _____.
PLURAL NOUN

Wearing your ring daily can cause subtle wear and tear over time.

Make a habit of cleaning it regularly by soaking it in _____
ADJECTIVE

water with a smidge of liquid _____. Leave it in there for no
NOUN

less than _____ minutes to allow the _____ particles
NUMBER   NOUN

to loosen up. Then, use a/an _____-brush and _____
PART OF THE BODY   ADVERB

scrub around the stone. Dip it again in the _____, then pat
TYPE OF LIQUID

dry with a soft _____. As a rule, try not to wear your bling
NOUN

when you're doing housework like washing the _____. Do
PLURAL NOUN

the _____ holding your diamond look bent out of shape? Get
PLURAL NOUN

thee to a jeweler at once! You'll _____ escape having to search
ADVERB

every nook and _____ of your house for a missing diamond.
NOUN

Or worse, your pet _____ might mistake your rock for kibble!
ANIMAL

MAD LIBS® is fun to play with friends, but you can also play it by yourself! To begin with, DO NOT look at the story on the page below. Fill in the blanks on this page with the words called for. Then, using the words you have selected, fill in the blank spaces in the story. Now you've created your own hilarious MAD LIBS® game!

PLURAL NOUN _____

NOUN _____

VERB _____

ADJECTIVE _____

NOUN _____

COLOR _____

FIRST NAME (FEMALE) _____

NOUN _____

FIRST NAME (MALE) _____

PART OF THE BODY _____

PLURAL NOUN _____

NOUN _____

NOUN _____

NOUN _____

VERB _____

PLURAL NOUN _____

Adult MAD LIBS®

The world's greatest _wedding_ game

ADDRESSING THE DRESS

After spending countless _____ picking out the perfect

PLURAL NOUN

wedding dress, you're left with a pricy piece of _____

NOUN

you're never going to _____ again. Then you pay a/an

VERB

_____ fortune to have it cleaned, only to stuff it in a/an

ADJECTIVE

_____ for eternity! Bummer, right? Not if you give your

NOUN

little _____ number a second chance at life! If you dropped a

COLOR

boatload of cash on a luxe brand like _____ Wang, you can

FIRST NAME (FEMALE)

recoup some moolah by selling it to another _____-to-be.

NOUN

Post an ad on _____-slist or on a second-_____ dress

FIRST NAME (MALE) — PART OF THE BODY

site. If you don't want to part with your beloved dress, try an arts

-and-_____ idea for turning it into a master-_____!

PLURAL NOUN — NOUN

You could take a piece of fabric and make a throw _____. Or

NOUN

you could sew a quilt for your marital _____. Some women

NOUN

take great pleasure in having a/an "_____ the dress" party,

VERB

where they wear it out on the town without a care in the world. Hey,

it'll make for some wild snap-_____ at the very least!

PLURAL NOUN

GIFT ROUNDUP

The world's greatest _wedding_ game

MAD LIBS® is fun to play with friends, but you can also play it by yourself! To begin with, DO NOT look at the story on the page below. Fill in the blanks on this page with the words called for. Then, using the words you have selected, fill in the blank spaces in the story. Now you've created your own hilarious MAD LIBS® game!

PLURAL NOUN _____

PLURAL NOUN _____

VERB ENDING IN "ING" _____

ADJECTIVE _____

VERB _____

PLURAL NOUN _____

PART OF THE BODY (PLURAL) _____

NOUN _____

ADJECTIVE _____

NOUN _____

NOUN _____

LETTER OF THE ALPHABET _____

NOUN _____

ADJECTIVE _____

NUMBER _____

NOUN _____

Adult MAD LIBS® GIFT ROUNDUP

The world's greatest _wedding_ game

Did your wedding _____ buy you stuff that wasn't on
PLURAL NOUN

your registry? Are you saddled with multiple crock-_____,
PLURAL NOUN

and you don't even cook? Get the gear you really want with our

gift-_____ strategy! One easy and _____ solution
VERB ENDING IN "ING" ADJECTIVE

is to practice the art of re-gifting. Between _____-days,
VERB

holidays, and weddings, you can easily pawn off one of your crystal

_____ to an unsuspecting recipient. If you've got some
PLURAL NOUN

time on your _____, track down which stores sell your
PART OF THE BODY (PLURAL)

unwanted items. Then, speak to a customer sales _____
NOUN

and ask if you can get store credit. If so, it's your _____ day!
ADJECTIVE

Exchange that _____-themed cheese platter for something less
NOUN

tacky. Like a/an _____-themed cheese platter! You can always
NOUN

try to sell things on _____-bay. If you just want the goods
LETTER OF THE ALPHABET

out of the house, make a/an _____-deductible donation to
NOUN

your local _____-will shop. For the right price, someone out
ADJECTIVE

there is just dying to own your _____-piece collection of
NUMBER

_____ figurines!
NOUN

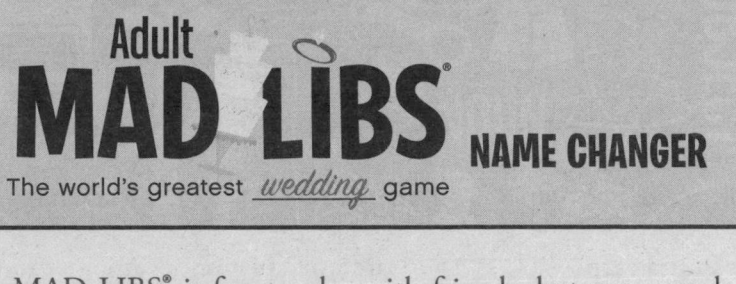

MAD LIBS® is fun to play with friends, but you can also play it by yourself! To begin with, DO NOT look at the story on the page below. Fill in the blanks on this page with the words called for. Then, using the words you have selected, fill in the blank spaces in the story. Now you've created your own hilarious MAD LIBS® game!

PLURAL NOUN _____

ADJECTIVE _____

A PLACE _____

NOUN _____

NOUN _____

NOUN _____

SAME NOUN _____

VERB _____

NOUN _____

NOUN _____

PART OF THE BODY _____

PART OF THE BODY (PLURAL) _____

COLOR _____

ADJECTIVE _____

With all of my former boy-_____, and okay, even with guys I
PLURAL NOUN

just had _____ crushes on, I would try on how their last names
ADJECTIVE

sounded with my first name. For a long stretch, I was infatuated with

being Mrs. Justin Timber-_____! I mean, who wasn't? Let's
A PLACE

face it, I've always been eager to ditch my name. Growing up with a

moniker like _____-butz has only caused me grief! Imagine my
NOUN

dismay when upon meeting the _____ of my dreams, I learn
NOUN

his last name is none other than _____-schitz! Really? So now
NOUN

I'm Mrs. _____-schitz. It's unclear if this is a/an _____
SAME NOUN   VERB

up or down from my old name. My husband says I must love him to

the end of the _____ and back to take his name. When we
NOUN

signed our _____ license and I officially changed my name,
NOUN

the registrar was all, "You know it's a pain in the _____ to
PART OF THE BODY

switch back once you do this, right?" I gritted my _____
PART OF THE BODY (PLURAL)

and politely told her I was aware of all the _____ tape involved
COLOR

with my decision. Call me _____, but I have to admit, it's
ADJECTIVE

starting to grow on me!

MAD LIBS® is fun to play with friends, but you can also play it by yourself! To begin with, DO NOT look at the story on the page below. Fill in the blanks on this page with the words called for. Then, using the words you have selected, fill in the blank spaces in the story. Now you've created your own hilarious MAD LIBS® game!

NOUN _____

PLURAL NOUN _____

VERB _____

VERB _____

ADJECTIVE _____

PLURAL NOUN _____

ADJECTIVE _____

NOUN _____

PLURAL NOUN _____

VERB ENDING IN "ING" _____

VERB _____

PLURAL NOUN _____

NOUN _____

VERB _____

NUMBER _____

ADJECTIVE _____

HONEY-DO LIST

The world's greatest _wedding_ game

Are you and your spouse newly living under the same _____?

NOUN

Believe it or not, a lot of couples argue about who is responsible

for household _____. Nobody wants to fight about whose

PLURAL NOUN

turn it is to _____ underneath the bed. It's a huge buzz-

VERB

_____ on the whole "just married" vibe! And yet, figuring out

VERB

a system is crucial for maintaining a/an _____ home. Make

ADJECTIVE

sure you both agree on a fair division of _____ before things

PLURAL NOUN

turn _____! First, each make a list of stuff you kind of enjoy

ADJECTIVE

doing and stuff you'd rather not touch with a ten-foot _____.

NOUN

Hey, you might discover that your honey is totally into folding

the _____ or _____ the toilet! Then, volunteer to

PLURAL NOUN VERB ENDING IN "ING"

do the chores that don't make you want to curl up in a corner and

_____. Of course, there might be some tasks that just plain

VERB

suck _____, like scrubbing _____ off the shower

PLURAL NOUN NOUN

curtain. Blech! Take turns, or, if you're feeling risky, _____

VERB

a coin! As long as you're engaged in a/an _____-way

NUMBER

conversation, you're off to a/an _____ start!

ADJECTIVE

Adult
MAD LIBS®
DECORATE OR DONATE?

The world's greatest _wedding_ game

MAD LIBS® is fun to play with friends, but you can also play it by yourself! To begin with, DO NOT look at the story on the page below. Fill in the blanks on this page with the words called for. Then, using the words you have selected, fill in the blank spaces in the story. Now you've created your own hilarious MAD LIBS® game!

NUMBER _____

NOUN _____

PLURAL NOUN _____

ADJECTIVE _____

VERB ENDING IN "ING" _____

VERB _____

ANIMAL _____

NOUN _____

NOUN _____

ADVERB _____

NOUN _____

PLURAL NOUN _____

NOUN _____

VERB ENDING IN "ING" _____

COLOR _____

ADJECTIVE _____

NOUN _____

Adult MAD LIBS

DECORATE OR DONATE?

The world's greatest _wedding_ game

Moving in together often means you've got _____ times
                                              NUMBER

the stuff to cram into your _____. Plus, all those wedding
                                 NOUN

_____ need space, too! Learn how to negotiate with each
 PLURAL NOUN

other about what stays and what goes. Make a list prioritizing

the items you are _____ to the grave, and those that you
                   VERB ENDING IN "ING"

are willing to _____ to the curb. This is not the time to
                 VERB

be a pack-_____! Consider the _____ footage and
            ANIMAL   NOUN

layout you have. Do you both claim to have the most comfortable

_____ ever but only have room for one? It's time
  NOUN

to _____ weed out redundant pieces of _____.
    ADVERB   NOUN

Make no _____ about it, you're going to have to sacrifice
         PLURAL NOUN

some of your beloved objects. Recognize that your Cabbage Patch

_____ collection may need to be retired. Oh, and the _Dirty_
  NOUN

_____ poster. There is a/an _____ lining, though . . .
 VERB ENDING IN "ING"   COLOR

your honey will also need to sift through his belongings with a/an

_____-toothed comb. This is the perfect time to finally get
  ADJECTIVE

rid of that _____ wall "art" you despise so much!
             NOUN

Adult MAD LIBS® FIGHTING RIGHT

The world's greatest _wedding_ game

MAD LIBS® is fun to play with friends, but you can also play it by yourself! To begin with, DO NOT look at the story on the page below. Fill in the blanks on this page with the words called for. Then, using the words you have selected, fill in the blank spaces in the story. Now you've created your own hilarious MAD LIBS® game!

NOUN _____

PLURAL NOUN _____

VERB ENDING IN "ING" _____

PLURAL NOUN _____

VERB ENDING IN "ING" _____

NOUN _____

VERB ENDING IN "ING" _____

ADJECTIVE _____

VERB ENDING IN "ING" _____

VERB _____

NOUN _____

ADJECTIVE _____

PLURAL NOUN _____

PART OF THE BODY (PLURAL) _____

PLURAL NOUN _____

ADJECTIVE _____

COLOR _____

Adult MAD LIBS® FIGHTING RIGHT

The world's greatest _wedding_ game

While you and your pookie-_____ will always be love-
                               NOUN

_____, it doesn't mean you won't have the occasional
   PLURAL NOUN

tiff. Stresses like _____ together and dealing with
                    VERB ENDING IN "ING"

the in-_____ are common causes for fights. Keep your
      PLURAL NOUN

_____ words fair with these tips, and no one will have
VERB ENDING IN "ING"

to sleep on the pull-out _____! First of all, figure out
                          NOUN

what you're really _____ about. It's easy to get into a/an
                   VERB ENDING IN "ING"

_____ cycle of petty arguments without addressing what
ADJECTIVE

the under-_____ issue is. Instead of keeping resentment
          VERB ENDING IN "ING"

inside, _____ to the chase with your sweetie. Clear the
        VERB

_____ with a frank, _____-headed conversation
NOUN   ADJECTIVE

about what's bothering you. Try to keep _____ from running
                                        PLURAL NOUN

high! A gentle, _____-on approach will help make tension
                PART OF THE BODY (PLURAL)

disappear. Also, it's important to pick your _____. Addressing
                                              PLURAL NOUN

every perceived _____-doing will only leave you seeing
                ADJECTIVE

_____!
COLOR

From ADULT MAD LIBS®: Just Married Mad Libs • Copyright © 2014 by Penguin Random House LLC.

The world's greatest _wedding_ game

MAD LIBS® is fun to play with friends, but you can also play it by yourself! To begin with, DO NOT look at the story on the page below. Fill in the blanks on this page with the words called for. Then, using the words you have selected, fill in the blank spaces in the story. Now you've created your own hilarious MAD LIBS® game!

VERB ENDING IN "ING" _____

NUMBER _____

NOUN _____

ADJECTIVE _____

NUMBER _____

ADJECTIVE _____

COLOR _____

PLURAL NOUN _____

NOUN _____

PART OF THE BODY _____

PART OF THE BODY _____

VERB _____

ADJECTIVE _____

PART OF THE BODY _____

VERB _____

PLURAL NOUN _____

ADJECTIVE _____

VERB _____

Adult MAD LIBS®

OLD-TIMER TALK

The world's greatest _wedding_ game

Me and my hunk of _____ love have been married for
VERB ENDING IN "ING"

_____ decades! Can you believe it? I tell ya, sometimes I
NUMBER

still feel like a blushing _____, the way my husband gives
NOUN

me the once over. I get a kick that he still thinks I'm _____
ADJECTIVE

stuff after all these years! For all you just-marrieds out there, rule

numero _____ to keeping things _____ in the sack
NUMBER   ADJECTIVE

is don't fall into a routine! It'll make your marriage duller than dry

_____ toast. What other _____ of wisdom do I have
COLOR   PLURAL NOUN

for you? Oh! That whole "don't go to sleep angry" stuff is a load of

horse-_____. You can go to bed wanting to rip your honey's
NOUN

_____ off, but make sure you work things out the next day.
PART OF THE BODY

Boy, I can't stand couples that are joined at the _____. You
PART OF THE BODY

need room to _____ when you're in it for the _____
VERB   ADJECTIVE

haul! Plus, absence really does make the _____ grow fonder.
PART OF THE BODY

After a _____-away with my girlfriends, I'm ready to jump
VERB

my hubby's _____! Want to know the real secret to a/an
PLURAL NOUN

_____-lasting marriage? _____ with the punches!
ADJECTIVE   VERB

Adult MAD LIBS® — BRIDE OR BUST

The world's greatest _wedding_ game

MAD LIBS® is fun to play with friends, but you can also play it by yourself! To begin with, DO NOT look at the story on the page below. Fill in the blanks on this page with the words called for. Then, using the words you have selected, fill in the blank spaces in the story. Now you've created your own hilarious MAD LIBS® game!

NUMBER _____

ADJECTIVE _____

PLURAL NOUN _____

VERB _____

ADJECTIVE _____

PLURAL NOUN _____

NOUN _____

ADJECTIVE _____

NUMBER _____

PLURAL NOUN _____

NOUN _____

VERB ENDING IN "ING" _____

FIRST NAME (MALE) _____

PLURAL NOUN _____

VERB _____

PART OF THE BODY (PLURAL) _____

Every time my family gets an invitation for another one of my

weddings, I always hear the same thing: "Didn't you just walk

down the aisle ＿＿＿＿＿ months ago?" And to them I explain,

NUMBER

＿＿＿＿＿ love has really found me this time. Besides, I

ADJECTIVE

always have an open bar at the reception, so stop getting your

＿＿＿＿＿ in a twist. It's true, I've promised to "till death

PLURAL NOUN

do us ＿＿＿＿＿" more times than I care to admit. My first

VERB

marriage was to my high-school ＿＿＿＿＿-heart. That lasted

ADJECTIVE

about as long as a carton of ＿＿＿＿＿. Then Number Two

PLURAL NOUN

was busted for ＿＿＿＿＿ fraud. Oops! And Number 3? The

NOUN

＿＿＿＿＿-life ＿＿＿＿＿-timed me! Number 4 was loaded,

ADJECTIVE　　　　NUMBER

but he bored me to ＿＿＿＿＿. What can I say? I got swept up in

PLURAL NOUN

the fantasy of ＿＿＿＿＿-trotting and jet-＿＿＿＿＿. After six

NOUN　　　　VERB ENDING IN "ING"

months, I said "Next!" Which brings me to Number 5, my darling

＿＿＿＿＿. I met him on Single-＿＿＿＿＿.com! He's smart

FIRST NAME (MALE)　　　　PLURAL NOUN

and makes me laugh until I ＿＿＿＿＿ in my pants! I think this

VERB

one's gonna stick. ＿＿＿＿＿ crossed!

PART OF THE BODY (PLURAL)

EASY ENTERTAINING

The world's greatest _wedding_ game

MAD LIBS® is fun to play with friends, but you can also play it by yourself! To begin with, DO NOT look at the story on the page below. Fill in the blanks on this page with the words called for. Then, using the words you have selected, fill in the blank spaces in the story. Now you've created your own hilarious MAD LIBS® game!

NOUN _____

ADJECTIVE _____

PART OF THE BODY (PLURAL) _____

NOUN _____

VERB _____

TYPE OF LIQUID _____

NOUN _____

NOUN _____

PART OF THE BODY _____

NOUN _____

VERB ENDING IN "ING" _____

PLURAL NOUN _____

A PLACE _____

VERB ENDING IN "ING" _____

ADJECTIVE _____

FIRST NAME (FEMALE) _____

You finally got your best wedding picture hung up on the

_____. You've got tons of brand-_____ kitchen
　　　NOUN　　　　　　　　　　　　　　　　　　　　　ADJECTIVE

gadgets to try out. And you haven't laid _____ on your
　　　　　　　　　　　　　　　　　　　PART OF THE BODY (PLURAL)

besties since the wedding. Which means it's time to host your first

dinner party as husband and _____! _____ up a guest
　　　　　　　　　　　　　　　NOUN　　　　　　VERB

list with your partner. If you have a few friends that get along like

oil and _____, then obviously don't ask them both. Divvy
　　　　TYPE OF LIQUID

up pre-party chores like setting the _____ and fishing stray
　　　　　　　　　　　　　　　　　　NOUN

pieces of _____ out of the couch cushions. Make recipes
　　　　　NOUN

that you know like the back of your _____. This is not the
　　　　　　　　　　　　　　　　PART OF THE BODY

time to bust out braised _____ if you've never touched a
　　　　　　　　　　　　　NOUN

_____ pan before!
VERB ENDING IN "ING"

As your friends arrive, have finger _____ out for nibbling. Put
　　　　　　　　　　　　　　　　PLURAL NOUN

your spouse on "guest duty" to make everyone feel like they're at (the)

_____. While they mingle, you can add the _____
A PLACE　　　　　　　　　　　　　　　　　　　　VERB ENDING IN "ING"

touches to your meal! Keep the vibe _____-key. Bickering is a
　　　　　　　　　　　　　　　ADJECTIVE

definite _____ Downer!
FIRST NAME (FEMALE)